MIDDLE SCHOOL
How to Deal

MIDDLE SCHOOL
How to Deal

By Sara Borden, Sarah Miller, Alex Stikeleather,
Maria Valladares, and Miriam Yelton

With a foreword by Karen Bokram
Editor-in-Chief of
GIRLS' LIFE MAGAZINE

Illustrated by Yuki Hatori

chronicle books · san francisco

A special thanks goes out to Jan Martí for volunteering her *professional* skills
and Bruce Borden and Judy Stikeleather for their fabulous technical help.
Thanks also to Amy Smart, Malcolm Harris, Max Fox, and Jon Gui and our
devoted mothers: Laura Borden, Megan Miller, Judy Stikeleather, Edelmira
Alcazar, and Melanie Yelton. Last but not least, we want to thank each other
for being an amazing team of girlfriends on an awesome school project.

Text © 2005 by Sara Borden, Sarah Miller, Alex Stikeleather,
Maria Valladares, and Miriam Yelton.
Illustrations © 2005 by Chronicle Books LLC.

Book design by Kristine Brogno.
Typeset in Neutra and August Medium.
Illustrations by Yuki Hatori / CWC International, Inc. (www.cwc-i.com)
The illustrations in this book were rendered digitally.
Manufactured in Canada.

Library of Congress Cataloging-in-Publication Data
Middle school: how to deal / by Sara Borden
... [et al.] ;
illustrated by Yuki Hatori.
p. cm.
Includes bibliographical references and index.
ISBN 0-8118-4497-8 (pbk); ISBN 0-8118-4845-0 (library binding)
1. Middle schools—Humor. 2. Middle school students—
Attitudes. I.
Borden, Sara.
LB1623.M523 2005
373.236—dc22
2004010822

Distributed in Canada by Raincoast Books
9050 Shaughnessy Street, Vancouver, British Columbia V6P 6E5

10 9 8 7 6 5 4 3 2

Chronicle Books LLC
85 Second Street, San Francisco, California 94105

www.chroniclekids.com

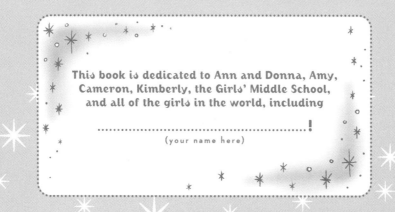

This book is dedicated to Ann and Donna, Amy, Cameron, Kimberly, the Girls' Middle School, and all of the girls in the world, including

....!

(your name here)

CONTENTS

Your World

Your Body and You

Good-bye and Good Luck!

My Middle School Notes

FOREWORD FROM GIRLS' LIFE MAGAZINE

Middle school. It's not high school yet, but it's definitely not your old grammar school either, right? Suddenly, instead of having one teacher all day, every day, you're switching classes every period. There are loads of class assignments to stay on top of. Cool new peeps to meet and greet. Your friends are changing—and (whoops!)—so's your bod. Not to mention that you *still* have no idea where to sit in the cafeteria.

I know you're one smart cookie, and you're totally looking forward to this major new stage in your life. But you're also a *leetle,* um, worried. Unless you have a cool older friend or sister to clue you in, how are you supposed to know what to expect? A girl needs a little guidance from someone who knows what's up!

Have no fear. That's where *Middle School: How to Deal* comes in. Five totally real girls—Sara, Sarah, Alex, Maria, and Miriam—have stepped up to help you navigate your new sitch. They've got a whole book full of tips and advice on how to master the new world of the middle school: juggling more classwork, keeping your fam life on an even keel, getting set with the changes in your growing body, staying out of the popularity trap, snagging an awesome, diverse group of buds, and—of course—dealing with the mysterious and sometimes elusive boyfriend (or is he your *boy friend*?).

This isn't just an advice book—it's crucial knowledge that will keep you sailing smoothly through the halls without getting sucked under by all the new and strange changes life is bringing ya right now.

But the best part is, *Middle School* isn't written by someone who last set foot in middle school a million years ago. It's a book by the best experts of all—real-life middle-school girls who *just went through* all the stuff you're about to face! Even better, you won't just hear from one girl—you're going to get the totally true stories, advice, and deep-down dish from a whole group of cool girls who've got smarts, expertise, and experience to spare.

So get psyched to figure out what's waiting for you on that first day—and for the next two or three years of your life. Just think—a little while from now, instead of wondering where the cafeteria could possibly have gotten to, *you*'ll be the expert helping all the other newbies find their place in the middle-school pack.

What could be cooler than that?

Love,

Karen Bokram

Editor-in-Chief & Publisher, *Girls' Life Magazine*

HELLO THERE!

The book that you are holding in your hands was written by five really serious, extremely wise, incredibly talented, and amazingly mature (hahaha) seventh grade girls. We decided to write a fab-a-licious book that's all about the things we wish we'd known when *we* were grade school kids about to go to middle school. In other words, we seventh graders wrote this book for girls like you, so you can learn from our mistakes! We survived the incredible transition from grade school to middle school, and we'll tell you about the important stuff that we learned the hard way, from how to take notes to how to take off your bra without taking off your shirt—a great trick for locker rooms! Sounds cool, huh? That's cuz it is!!

Welcome to middle school!

Love and hugs (and kisses),
Sara Borden, Sarah Miller, Alex Stikeleather,
Maria Valladares, and Miriam Yelton
**We are not professional writers,
but we *were* professional middle schoolers!!**

THE WORLD OF MIDDLE SCHOOL

Good-bye, Grade School...Hell-o, Middle School!

Advancing from one grade to another is a **big** deal. Whether you're going from kindergarten to first grade or from fourth grade to fifth, it's an exciting and important change in your life. But when you move into sixth grade (or maybe seventh grade, depending on your school system), you're not just moving from one grade to the next. You're leaving elementary school behind and stepping into that scary new place called middle school. Where you live it might even be called junior high. Now that's a change that's really big!

Elementary school was this safe little haven where you were with the same people for six to seven years. Except for having music or art on some days, you had the same schedule every day of the week, and you stayed with the same teacher for the whole day. It was all pretty consistent and routine.

But then time flew, and before you knew it, you were in a nice dress making a speech at graduation! You were saying good-bye to grade school, that old familiar place, forever, and moving on to middle school—a whole different world.

In middle school, you'll probably have a different teacher for every subject, different kids in every class, and different things to challenge you each and every day! Middle school is a bumbling, jumbling, mixed-up place of classes, friends, boyfriends, and activities. It's a jungle out there!

This can be a very scary experience, and you're probably wondering what it'll be like. You know, being separated from your best pal, having lots of new teachers, and crushing on that cute guy who sits in front of you in geography (man, don't you just love his haircut?). Soon you'll be in a world where everyone—parents, teachers, friends, guys—expects way more of you than they did when you lived in your safe old grade school world. But as overwhelming as all these changes seem, they are perfectly normal.

And being scared of these changes is normal, too. We're all afraid of change. But if you know what changes are going to happen, they're usually not as bad, because you're prepared to face them head on. So read on and go get 'em, Tiger!

The First Day

So, summer vacation is over. You've bought all of your supplies, the matching binder and backpack, and number 2 pencils. You also went shopping with your friends and so of course you have the totally cute first-day outfit. You're ready for the first day of middle school.

You walk through the doors of your new school and see all of these people: punks, Martha Stewarts, jocks, everyone. What do you do?

If you see people you know, you're in luck—you can just walk over and start swapping summer stories. But if you don't know anyone, you might be tempted to just go sit down by yourself. Don't!! A better choice is to sit next to someone who looks friendly. It's totally normal to be shy. But middle school is a new beginning, so you might as well start it off right. Go ahead and put yourself out there: Make the first move, even if all you do is say "hi!" If you're not used to speaking up and making new friends, this can be a scary transition, but you'll have to make these transitions in life all the time. You can do it! You just have to get prepared and have fun. The best way to do this is to **have self-confidence!** People are attracted to self-confidence. Not arrogance, but confidence. Just **be yourself** and have faith in yourself—faith that you can learn, make new friends, and succeed. You know the expression "Seeing is believing"? Well sometimes, you need to believe in order to see.

The Popularity Trap

In middle school, you may discover that popularity isn't just a contest—it can be a full-on war! Popularity is a really big deal in middle schools. Most times, there is one major popular group on campus, or sometimes two. Usually these are the kids who have boyfriends and lots of friends, and who everybody else wishes they were (bad idea). Often, popular cliques are excluding or, worse, Extremely Evil. Why do we let our popular peers run the show and set our standards for cool?

Two girls give their opinions on popularity:

MICHELLE

Q. *Why do you think the popular kids are allowed to rule the show?*
A. *I think one of the reasons could be that there are qualities in people that are real leadership qualities, and I think that a fair amount of the popular people have that quality, even if they use their power in a mean/evil way.*

CAMBRIA

Q. *Do you think that the popular kids should get away with running the show?*
A. *No, I don't. When a small group of kids are given the power over the entire grade, you only get one point of view setting the standards for the entire grade. In a perfect world, everybody would be able to set their standards for themselves.*

We agree. We think it's really boring and messed up for one group of kids to run everybody else's lives! You should express yourself openly without feeling intimidated by others, and if you're going to impress people, impress them by being yourself. If you really like someone's sense of style, it's okay to let yourself be inspired by her. But be very careful not to change because of people who try to make you feel you're not good enough the way you are. This is a big mistake that a lot of girls, and boys, too, can make.

Why do we let people change how we dress, talk, act, or think? Maybe it's because we don't like who we are, or we think *they* don't like who we are (and maybe they don't, but why should we care?). Either way, we do it because we want to be accepted. And maybe you will be accepted if you completely change who you are. But guess what? It'll all be just an act. The person that people *think* they like won't really be you at all, so you'll be constantly on your guard and hiding your true self. Plus, once you let someone change how you act, you're giving them the power to control how you treat other people and interact with them, how you do in school, and maybe even how you think. Nobody's acceptance is worth that.

Being yourself is so important. This is one thing we really want to stress. You have to live with yourself for the rest of your life, so you might as well learn to love yourself now. And no matter what people may say, there isn't anything wrong with you!

Don't believe us? Read on!

CARRI'S STORY

At my school, the popular kids ruled the show. They set all the standards for everything. Everyone wanted to be part of their group. It wasn't that easy, though. You had to have a boyfriend, be pretty, wear a bra, make fun of "nerdy losers," and even leave your other friends if the popular group didn't like them. I made that mistake. I left the friends that had cared about me, played with me, and hung out with me for five years. I tried the popular gang. For a while, it was so great! I felt so powerful, so loved! But eventually, the leader got tired of me. I was no longer the newest, hippest thing, the new girl that they could just mold into what they wanted. The rest of the gang followed her example, as usual, and they all turned on me. It was so horrible! That was when I realized what a mistake I'd made, and that my old friends were the ones who really cared about me. The summer came, and so did a new school year. Now I'm at a new school with a new set of friends. I know they are my friends, because they haven't tried to change me, and they don't care how I look or dress. They don't care who I hang out with when I'm not with them or if I have a boyfriend or not. They like me for me.

SONYA'S STORY

The popular crowd at my school was known as the "preppies."
They wore designer clothing, spent money, and mostly knew each
other from the expensive sport camps they all went to. During the
first week of sixth grade, my circle of good friends from elemen-
tary school gathered together at lunch under the oak tree, while
the preppies hung out by the bleachers. We were chatting and
eating lunch when my friend Sarah cleared her throat and
announced, "Guys, I think it's time we tried hanging out with other
people, not just each other, so I'm not going to be here tomorrow
at lunchtime." I was okay with making new friends, but I knew
what Sarah meant. Over the summer she hadn't wanted to hang
out with the rest of us as much. Instead she had been calling up
some of the more popular girls and going shopping with them. I
personally didn't want to buy a whole new wardrobe just to have
friends! The next day, about half our group of friends split: some
went off with Sarah to the bleachers, the rest of us stayed under
the oak tree. At first my friends (or what was left of them) were
bummed out, but we got over it and made new friends that liked
us for who we were, and not the labels on our shirts.

School Dances

Dancing—sounds like fun, doesn't it? But let us warn you, school dances can be very stressful events.

Middle school is where you usually have your first real dance. It all starts with the outfit. What are you going to wear? What outfit will make guys want to dance with you?

We bet by now you know exactly what we're going to say, right? **Just be yourself!** Guys should like you for you; if they don't, they're not worth worrying about. So forget wearing a tight little skirt or a tube top, and don't even consider padding your bra! When we say be yourself, we mean it! Wear something that makes you feel you look your best but is still comfortable and easy to dance in. And dress to be cool—in temperature, that is. Even if the dance is during winter, wear something light (but bring a sweater) because it can get really warm at dances and you don't want to end up sweating like a racehorse.

The next thing you're probably thinking is, "Omigosh—I look like a freak when I dance. What should I do?" Don't worry; just go. A lot of people can't dance but just sort of move around to the music. Confidence is the key. If you are confident and smiling, no matter how you dance, all people will be thinking is, "Wow! She looks like she's having fun!" Soon enough, you'll be having such a good time, going crazy to the funky beat and laughing with your friends, that you'll never want it to be over. Score!

On the other hand, you could find yourself wanting to cry and not knowing why. Maybe you start liking a cute guy right there on the dance floor, but so does everyone else. Maybe the guy you like is acting as if *he* likes your worst enemy or, even worse, your best friend! At dances, hormones are buzzing around like a swarm of bees, so someone is bound to get stung. If that someone is you, remember that you are an amazing, confident girl with a great personality. Try to forget the hurt and just have fun. There will be other dances and other boys you'll want to dance with! Don't let it tear you up—or tear up your relationship with your girlfriends.

Diversity Is Cool!

As you get older, you start to notice differences in people: race, personality traits, physical characteristics, and religious beliefs. Everyone looks and acts different and has different opinions about things. Because of this, diversity is a gift—it's a way for people to teach one another new things. It is what makes the world so interesting. How cool is it to think that everyone is unique in her own way and that that's the way it should be! If everyone were the same, life would be very boring. It's each person's responsibility to respect and honor one another's differences.

Read what one very coolio Latina girl has to say about diversity!

MARIA'S STORY

For me, diversity is a big issue because being Latina, I find it hard to succeed mentally because of stereotypes. Throughout my time in middle school, I felt that I was alone, although friends surrounded me. I guess I felt alone because I was one of the only Latina girls at my school. I couldn't speak Spanish with them and discuss my life, because they had been raised differently than I had, and I was afraid they would judge me based on that. I never felt that people were at ease when they talked with me. They tried to "speak my language" by imitating what they saw on TV. I felt that most of my classmates were afraid that I would hurt them or something. I guess what I wanted was someone I could be around who wouldn't try to "talk" like me and talk down to me. I wish that we had more diversity so everyone would get over the stereotypes and learn to see people for who they really are. With more diversity we would get to know more about other people's cultures and their ways of life and would not be afraid to get to know them better.

Speaking Up in Class

Have you ever had a great idea (or even a not-so-great idea) in class but been afraid to say anything? Why do you think that was? Well, here is a possibility: Maybe you were worried about what people would think of your ideas. More specifically, maybe you were worried about what *boys* would think of them. (Not that they have any better ideas!) You know boys, those cute creatures that are amazingly human—and amazingly distracting? Of course, this would not happen in certain environments. For example, it wouldn't happen at an all-girls school. No way, no how! So if you attend an all-girls school, remember that this is one of the super-cool things about your school. No boys to worry about!

If you go to a co-ed school (with girls and boys), you have to learn to forget that boys exist, at least during those moments when you have a great idea in class. There are some girls who are not afraid to speak their minds, no matter who is listening and watching. Boys do not affect what they say and do at all. However, for those who are affected (which is most of the middle school girl population), we have this advice: Your mission, double-O girl, is to stop worrying about what anyone else thinks and start caring more about what *you* think!! This can be a really tough change, but we know that any girl who puts her mind to it can do it.

Stressed Out! Tips and Advice to Help You Deal

So you're getting ready to give an important speech at school, or go to an important social event, and you're soooo stressed. You don't have a tube bra to wear under your tank top, your jeans have a ketchup stain on them, and you can't find your favorite glitter body wash! You're missing one of your note cards!! Nothing is going right.

What you need, of course, is the strength to realize that although these setbacks seem like a big deal, they're really not. They just feel that way right now because you're so stressed out. We can't give you this strength, but we can give you some great stress-busting tips to help **you** find the strength for yourself.

The key is to *relax*. We know: it's much easier said than done, but try some of our techniques on the next page. They work!

On the morning before you're going up in front of your entire class to give an oral report, try this method of relaxation:

1. Lie down on your bed, close your eyes, and take deep, long breaths.

2. Starting with the tips of your feet and moving up gradually, tense your entire body slowly. First squeeze your toes in against the balls of your feet. Then move your attention to your legs, tensing the muscles in your calves and thighs. Now tighten your bottomly-quarters, and squeeze your stomach muscles. Lock your elbows against your sides, and tense your shoulders. Squeeze your neck muscles, and tense your face. Squeeze your eyes shut. Continue to breathe deeply.

3. Hold your body tense for several moments. Then relax, feeling peace in your mind and body.

4. When you're ready, sit up slowly. Calmly review your notes for your speech. As you finish getting ready for school and doing any other pre-speech preparations, tell yourself that you're going to perform fabulously. Believe it and you will!

Another technique for calming yourself is visualization. Here are the steps:

1. Wherever you are, find a private space (if you can) and close your eyes. Take deep breaths. Focus on your breathing.

2. Next, focus on whatever you want to do well. It could be an algebra test or a basketball game. Imagine yourself getting an A or scoring the winning point. Imagine yourself being successful.

3. Once you're finished, slowly open your eyes. While you're taking your test or playing your game, keep that vision in your mind. Don't let it get in the way of answering a question correctly, or scoring points. Just let it sit in the back of your mind and inspire you.

Good luck with whatever you're stressing over! And don't forget to reach for the stars.

Classwork and Homework (Last—but Not Least!)

With all the other things going on, it sometimes may not seem like it, but the most important part of school is schoolwork! Believe it or not, you'll use what you learn in the first 18 years for the rest of your life. You'll use your knowledge to pass the SATs, to succeed in college, to write that annual report for your boss at your very first job (in the real world—YAY!!).

If you want to learn what your fine, upstanding educators have to teach you, it's important to pay attention and to take notes whenever you can. It's also important to do your homework—and turn it in on time. It's one thing if you have a family emergency or if your house burned down. But come on . . . my dog ate it? Aliens abducted me and took my math? My hamster peed on my English report? (Actually, that could happen . . .)

The point is, your teacher wouldn't give you homework if it was impossible to do. If you really feel like you have too much homework, or you need help on it, try talking to your parents and asking their advice. They'll help you come up with a plan. We can totally sympathize with you about the heavy homework load, but sometimes you just gotta pull your pants up like a big girl and roll with the punches of life. (After all, just think about what will happen to your social life if your parents find out you're not turning in your homework . . . say it with us: **grounded!**)

Here are some tips for getting the most out of class:

Listen to your teachers!! It is sooooo tempting to chat with your buddies, and the occasional note passing isn't that harmful, but try to keep your classtime socializing to a minimum, cuz when the teacher says, "Pop quiz!" you're going to be wishing that you had paid attention!

Take notes! Write down only the main points and important details. You won't be able to keep up if you write every single word that comes out of your teacher's mouth! It helps to abbreviate anything you can. Make sure to take notes even when your teacher doesn't say you have to, especially if you think the information is important. Eventually your teacher will stop reminding you, so it's good to get in the habit now.

Learn from the people around you who are smart, organized, and prepared. Others may classify these people as "nerds" (which is bad, as no one should be classified as anything except human beings!), but these are the students who take notes and pay attention. You would be wise to follow their example. Ask these students to share their tips for note-taking and other learning skills; they might have good strategies you can add to your own routine.

Now you have the skills you need in class, but what about studying on your own?

Think of study skills as a toolbox of ways to make learning the stuff you need to know a lot easier. Here are some studying and memorizing tips to help make tests and homework a breeze.

STUDYING

Some people learn best alone, while others learn best with a partner or in groups. Unfortunately, friends are often not the best study buddies because, well, you end up talking the whole time. If you must work with a partner, try working with someone at your level of understanding so you progress together. Agree on what you want to accomplish in your study session *before* you start, so you have a plan. And once you have a plan, stick to it!

MEMORY TRICKS

Memorizing is hard for about 99.9 percent of the population (the rest of you lucky ducks can skip this section and thank the gods for that amazing gift). But for the rest of us, memorizing can be the difference between an A and a grade that we won't even mention. The trick to memorizing is figuring how you remember things best. Some people remember things just by reading, writing, or saying them aloud over and over again. Others have to take a more interactive approach to learning by heart.

Here are a few tricks we recommend:

* Say what you need to memorize out loud.
* Write it in the air with your finger and visualize the info you're trying to commit to memory.
* Write a story using the information you're trying to memorize. (This is especially good for learning vocabulary.)
* Think of an acronym that will stand for what you're trying to memorize. (For example, HOMES is a handy way to remember Huron, Ontario, Michigan, Erie, and Superior, which are the Great Lakes!)
* Put the facts you need to know to a tune and make a song!

If you put them to use, all these tips and advice can help you succeed, which is a good thing if you don't want to be the expiration date tester at your local milk farm! To avoid this, we recommend you make learning at school your real priority ahead of crushes and socializing and popularity. Remember: Knowledge is power, and power is cool, and cool is fun. So therefore, knowledge is fun, in a twisted sort of way!

THE F'S OF LIFE:
FRIENDS, FAMILY—AND FOES!

Groups: Cool or Not?

The first week of middle school, many people hang back and are even quiet and shy. But after a week or two, people loosen up, become rowdy, and start making friends. This is when the groups or cliques start to emerge. You'll be able to see who the "geeks," the "jocks," the "popular ones," and the "loners" are, or whatever other labels you want to give them. This is also when people may start to feel excluded or hurt if they haven't really made friends or are not part of a group.

Whatever group you are part of, you have responsibilities. Let's say that you're part of one of the popular groups. Everyone wants to be your friend, people all love you, and you are known throughout the school. Great, right? Well, sometimes. When you're popular, you're in a position to hurt people emotionally, even without knowing it, so try not to be too exclusive, and take care to look out for other people's feelings. If there's someone you dislike because you think they're too needy or boring or whatever, you still should be nice. And remember, just because you are labeled with a stamp that says POPULAR doesn't mean you have to change yourself. You need to be you if you want to be "cool."

What if you are in a not-so-popular group? Well, that can actually be kind of good! You'll have more privacy, less pressure, and close friends within your group that you can do stuff with and nobody will care! However, you still have to be aware of people's feelings because (believe it or not) some people may want to be part of *your* group. But let's say you want to join the "popular group." If this group is mean and exclusive, don't do it—stick with your close buds! But if they are nice and inclusive, you probably have a chance. Try hanging out with them for a couple of days. Learn about what they enjoy doing and see if you enjoy doing the same stuff. If you don't, you probably shouldn't become friends with them.

Whatever you do, don't try to change your personality to be in the spotlight. Some people are leaders, some followers. You may need to accept the fact (if it is the fact) that you're more a follower than someone who likes to be out front leading. If you want to be the leader, though, just put yourself out there and go for it! Just because you're usually a leader or usually a follower doesn't mean you have to play that role in every situation. If you feel like switching things up sometimes, you can. It's your choice.

Finally, maybe you are part of NO group. You're a loner. (Aww, poor baby!) Well, like everything else, this has its ups and downs. One big "up" is that you can try hanging with all kinds of groups and then choose the one or several that suit you best. Or maybe you can find some other people that are not part of any group, and you guys can create your own crew.

Cliques are a big part of middle school, but it doesn't have to be a big part of your life. It doesn't matter if you are part of a group or not: It's just a label, and you're still you.

The Friendship Test

Every girl in the world has a different idea of what she wants her friends to be. There are no perfect friends! Friends have probably been a very important part of your life from the time you were a small kid, but when you enter middle school you may find they become a very difficult part of your life as well. Friendships in middle school seem to get more confusing and harder to handle than friendships in grade school. You'll go through a lot of big life events with your middle school friends, so it is very important to have friends that you like being with and trust. Friends should never force you into anything you don't want to do. They also should be loyal, trustworthy, and respectful. If they are going around telling all your secrets and not respecting you, then they aren't really worth it.

It's a good idea to think about what you need and want in a friend. Knowing what qualities are important to you will help you pick the best pals for *you*.

Check it if you got it!! THE FRIEND CHECKLIST!!

Do your friends treat you with R-E-S-P-E-C-T?
○ They honor your opinions
● They don't go blabbing things you don't want other people to know
○ They are kind to you
○ They treat you in a way that's true to who and what you are (a human for goodness' sake)

Are your friends loyal?
○ They give you honest, heartfelt advice
○ They always tell the truth
● They always stand up for ~~you~~ each other

Or are your friends using you? (Be strong and calm)
○ They don't talk or listen to you much
○ They boss you around
● They hang out with you only when it's convenient for them

That's the friend test! A true friend should have most if not all of the positive qualities listed above (and you should, too). And if they have those other qualities? Drop 'em!

BFFs

Best friends can be a wonderful, tricky, or just plain fun part of your life. You can have one best friend or several. It's also possible to *not* have a best friend; maybe you have one or two or a few tight friends and don't consider any of them your "best" pal.

What's the point of a best friend, then? Well, the point is to have someone you can have fun with, confide in, trust, and love. But it's important to know you can have all of this with people you consider just plain friends, too. So don't be bummed if you don't have a "best friend."

One of the most important things about having a best friend, or any friend, is treating them well. Friendships are all about give and take, so you have to do your share, and your friends have to do theirs. If they aren't doing their part, then you have to talk to them. If you're not doing your part, you should probably think about what you can do to make the friendship better.

Girl Talk: Lingo for Online Chats

In middle school, you'll probably find that you talk to your friends online as much as you talk to them on the phone, maybe more. Sometimes when we chat online, it's almost like a different language! So this is your handy translator full of our online code, including the most common usages and some that are just fun. Feel free to write new ones that you discover here, and don't be afraid to ask the person you're talking to what they mean!!

1	One		BTW	By the way
2	To/too		C	See
4eva	Forever		CUL	See you later
4get	Forget		CUZ	Because
404	I haven't a clue		CYA	See ya
AFK	Away from keyboard		DTRT	Do the right thing
ASAP	As soon as possible		DWB	Don't write back
B4N	Bye for now		F2T	Free to talk
BAK	Back at the keyboard		FAQ	Frequently asked question(s)
BB	Bye, bye		FYI	For your info
BBL	Be back later		G2G	Got to go
BBS	Be back soon		GF	Girlfriend
BF	Boyfriend		GFN	Gone for now
BFF	Best friend forever		G2GP	Gotta go pee
BRB	Be right back		GL	Good luck
BTDT	Been there, done that		GR8	Great

IMO	In my opinion		THANX	Thanks/thank you
JK	Just kidding		THO	Though
K	OK		THX	Thanks
L8R	Later		TTFN	Ta-ta for now
LOL	Laugh out loud/lots of love		TTT	Thought that, too (when someone types in what you were about to type)
LTNS	Long time no see			
LTR	Long-term relationship			
MAYB	Maybe		TTYL	Talk to you later
NM	Nothing much		TU	Thank you
NVM	Never mind		TY	Thank you
O	Oh		U	You
OIC	Oh, I see		UW	You're welcome
OMG	Oh my God		WAS^	What's up
OTF	On the phone		WAT	What
POAHF	Put on a happy face		WAYD	What are you doing?
POOF	Good-bye (leaving the room)		WB	Welcome back
POS	Parent over shoulder		WBS	Write back soon
QT	Cutie		WTF	What the frick
R	Are		WTG	Way to go!
S'up/SUP	What's up		WTV	Watching television
SRY	Sorry		WU?	What's up?
SUX	Sucks		Y	Why
SYS	See you soon		YA	Yeah/yes
TCOY	Take care of yourself		YW	You're welcome
TGIF	Thank God it's Friday		ZO	Zoning out

When Nothing Means Something

When you read that title, you probably thought, "What in the world does this have to do with being in middle school?" Well, the truth is, not much. But knowing what it means will help you deal with friends throughout the rest of your life!

Have you ever had a friend who seems stressed or mopey, but when you ask what's up she quickly answers "nothing" or "I'm fine"? The problem with this response is (1) it's probably not true, and (2) it doesn't give you any information or any way to help her. This response just makes you want to know what's going on even more, and there is a high chance that she gave you that response because deep down she really wants to tell you. However, sometimes "nothing" really does mean "nothing," or it means "something" but she truly doesn't want to talk about it. The trick is figuring out what "nothing" really means.

If you know the friend well, you may be able to tell right away whether she wants your help or wants you to bug off. If you don't know her well, you have to be tactful and considerate if you want to figure out what she's thinking.

In most instances, "nothing" is not a good response for either of you. If "nothing" means "something," she's basically asking you to give her "I'm the center of the world, look at me, poor me" attention. This kind of attitude doesn't accomplish anything (which is why, if you find yourself often answering "nothing," try saying, "Yes, there is something but I don't want to talk about it" or "Yes, there is something; please talk with me").

It's important for you to be supportive of this friend, but don't buy into this act for too long. To get to the bottom of her problems, try waiting until she's in a better mood and talking to her about why her "nothing" response makes being her friend difficult for you. She'll probably see your point of view. If she doesn't, the next time she says "nothing" you may have to just say "okay" and leave it at that. Just do what you believe is right, make sure that you take care of yourself, and don't overextend.

Fights

Fighting with a friend can feel like the worst thing ever. But fallouts with your friends don't have to end badly if, instead of yelling, screaming, and blaming, you guys just try to talk. Yes, we said talk. You know, communicate, converse, negotiate—and listen. You should listen to each other's side of the story, and try to compromise or see what one of you or both of you could have done differently. It is so much easier to talk it out than to hurt each other in some way. And it's always best to face problems head on and not let fights get worse and worse until it becomes "I'm not talking to you anymore" or "We can't be friends." That would suck! Isn't it *much* better to talk through the problem than to lose your bestest bud? Of course it is! So the moral of this story is: Talk instead of yell, and don't be afraid to have disagreements with your friends. Getting through them in a way that's honest, direct, and respectful will only make your friendship stronger!

Family Issues

Family is a very important part of your life, but it has its ups and downs, especially now that you're getting older, becoming more and more your own person, and thinking more independently. It may seem that your folks want you to be their baby the way you've always been. You may wish they'd just learn to leave you alone. But think about what it would be like if you didn't have your family. Hard to imagine, isn't it? No matter how big of a pain they are sometimes, your parents care about you, and they always will.

Everyone's family has fights. It may sound funny, but being able to argue and disagree is a very important part of being a family!

Disagreeing and arguing is okay—it's about expressing your feelings, and your family are the very people you should be able to express youself with honestly. But even when you fight, you have to be sensitive to your family members—*all* of your family members. First, you have to be respectful of whomever you're fighting with, whether it's your mom, dad, or annoying sib. At the time you're fighting it might be really hard to see, but they have feelings, too, and are probably just as mad, hurt, and annoyed as you are. Second, you have to be aware of the members of your family who aren't a part of this fight but will still probably be affected by it. Be kind to them, and try really hard to not to lash out at them just because you're angry.

In good times and bad, you'll always have a good relationship with your family if you communicate. When you communicate what you need or what's going on in your life, your family can help you, sometimes in surprising ways. They know a lot more than you think, and they can give you priceless advice. And even if you have a problem that your family can't solve, they can always listen, and that helps, too. Sometimes it's hard to talk with family members; learning to do so may be a skill that takes you a long time to develop. But don't give up! Talking to your family may not be as easy as you would like it to be, but if you keep trying, in the end it will all even out for you and for everyone.

Dealing with Bullies

No doubt about it: Bullies can be scary. They vary from the stereotypical bully who's big and looks tough to the mean, exclusive girls who rule the school. They can terrorize elementary schools, middle schools, high schools—even colleges!—and can hurt you physically, mentally, and emotionally if they're not stopped.

Why do bullies do what they do? They might go into the bully business because they feel insecure. Bullying makes them feel powerful and in charge. They also might enjoy the attention they receive from their bad deeds. Or maybe they're just jealous of you. Whatever the cause, don't think for even a second that you are to blame for being bullied! There is no excuse for one kid to terrorize another.

You probably have your own way of dealing with unpleasant people, but bullies are different. They can be more aggressive and meaner than your average person. You may have to try several different tactics to get bullies to back off. If you can, avoid them. Of course, that's not always possible, so you may have to try just ignoring them. If you can't ignore them at least don't let them get a rise out of you. After all, that's what they want.

As scary as it sounds, you might also try talking to them. Pull them aside and tell them that what they are doing is wrong. Tell them that they hurt your feelings and ask them to stop. Be firm and try not to look scared. Explain your position in a calm, reasonable tone of voice. If you stay strong and talk to them one on one—away from their friends and people they're trying to impress—you'll probably be able to reach them. You may not

become friends, but at least you can make peace and not have an enemy anymore. If that doesn't work, tell your parents, a teacher, or maybe even your school principal what is happening, and they can step in. No matter what, if bullies become more than you can handle, reach out and ask for help!

Interview with Actress AMY SMART

Amy Smart has starred in TV shows and movies with major actors including Jennifer Gardner, Ashton Kutcher, and Ben Stiller. She's proof that middle school can be challenging for everyone—even gorgeous girls who grow up to be successful actresses in Hollywood!

Q. *What do you wish you had known in middle school?*
A. *I wish I knew how beautiful my body was and that being flat-chested was wonderful, even though I got teased a lot.*

Q. *If you could have changed something about yourself in middle school, what would that be?*
A. *I wouldn't have changed anything because I was at where I was supposed to be at that time.*

Q. *What is one of your memories from middle school?*
A. *Playing Truth or Dare.*

Q. *When you were in middle school, what career did you think you were going to have when you grew up?*
A. *I thought I was going to be a hairdresser and teach at a ballet school. I thought I was too shy to be an actress. I thought I couldn't do it. This friend of mine was acting, and an example is stronger than ten thousand facts, and when I saw it I was inspired. I was 16.*

Q. *What is some advice you would give to kids moving into middle school?*
A. *The more you believe in yourself, the clearer it is to make your dreams happen. We're all special in our own ways.*

BOYS, BOYS, BOYS

What Boys Think (and Say!) About Girls

Boys have a totally different language than girls. Often guys just look at things in completely different ways than we do, so sometimes even when they mean to be nice or funny, what they say or do may be offensive instead! For example, you might tell a guy he has great hair and he'll really appreciate your compliment. However, if he tries to return the compliment by telling you that you have great boobs, you'll probably feel pretty offended! It's never okay for guys to make rude remarks, but it can be true that sometimes when boys really like you or have a crush on you, they may tease you, gross you out, and do or say stuff that girls think is totally evil. But actually, they're just trying to interact with you and get your attention. It's really confusing if you think about it, but it works!

Girl-to-girl note: This is true only up to a point! Don't fall for the myth that "boys will be boys" and can't control themselves. Of course they can! If a guy ever crosses the line, speak up! You'll feel good about standing up for yourself and he'll respect you for it, too. Keep reading to learn more about what boys think from the special creatures themselves!

We asked one of our guy friends his views about girls and relationships!

Q: *Do you think it's okay or good to have boy-girl relationships in middle school?*
A: *Of course!*

Q: *What's the thing you like most about relationships with girls?*
A: *The conversation.*

Q: *What's the thing you dislike most in girls?*
A: *Immaturity.*

Q: *Most important piece of advice for middle school girls?*
A: *Don't go out just because everyone else is!*

Next, we went to another buddy and asked him some different questions:

Q: *What good relationships or experiences do you remember having with girls in middle school?*
A: *Friends that were girls, and girlfriends.*

Q: *What made them good?*
A: *We could talk!*

Q: *What problems did you have?*
A: *Keeping in touch was a problem.*

Q: *Do you think you have the right to pressure a girl?*
A: *Yes, in a positive way. Like, pressure them to do things that are good for them. In a negative way, no.*

Q: *How important are brains, personality, and self-esteem in girls to you?*
A: *Pretty important!!*

Finally, we went to yet another guy pal and asked him some more questions:
Q: *How important are looks to you?*
A: *As important as [it is that] girls are to be fun with.*

Q: *What do you think about dating in middle school?*
A: *It's okay as long as it doesn't become a sexual thing.*

Q: *Are there things you dislike in girls?*
A: *If they're obnoxious or conceited or all stuck up!*

Q: *Do you think you have the right to pressure a girl?*
A: *Ugh, no . . .*

Q: *Any advice for middle school girls?*
A: *Be relaxed about dating and don't be so worried about what we think!*

There you have it!
Some pretty different opinions, from three very different, real live middle school guys!!

What's the Deal with Dating?

Ah yes, that magical subject of dating. The word you've grown up hearing from your older brothers and sisters, your friends, and the media. The subject (or one of them!) your parents are probably dreading the most. That means you shouldn't talk to them about it, right? **Wrong!** Your friends may be fun and easy to talk to, but your parents are the ones in the know. So talk. They'll listen.

It's important to discuss dating with your parents and find out what their rules and expectations are. But be warned: They won't always tell you what you want to hear! If you talk to them and they tell you not to date right now, then **don't**. Even if your friends are dating, resist the urge to ignore your parents' advice and just talk to your friends about this matter. Some of your friends may have

gone through this (a little bit), but it's not the same. Your parents have been here for a while, so they know some stuff. They went through this. Although you might like your friends' ideas better, your parents can give you much smarter advice on guys and dating. (Trust us on this one!)

If your parents *do* say you can date, take it slowly, one step at a time. Say you meet this totally perfect boy (actually, he could be better, but he's a guy, right?) and you have a major crush. It turns out he likes you back (score!). So what do you do? We suggest talking to him alone, away from his friends. Ask him why he likes you, whether he's gone out with a girl before, and if he's sure he wants to date and maybe be in a relationship. (No "I do" needed, though, babe!) If all signs point to YES, then go for it, girl! Our recommendation: Go to a smoothie shop, to the arcade, on a walk, or to the movies. And maybe hold hands. And that's it. Yes, we did just say that. Hey, it's a free country and you can do what you want, but you're in the sixth grade, honey. If you're planning on going farther (like kissing), talk to your mom first.

So this dating subject can be a bit of a roller coaster. Should I do it because my friends do? Should I not do it because my mom said no? Our main advice: Listen to your parents, listen to yourself, and do what you really think is right. Just remember: Things at this age don't last forever (often just for a few days or maybe a month, tops!). When you're eighteen, it'll be different! But for now, enjoy being young and carefree (and quite possibly Blissfully Single!) while it lasts.

Boy Friend or *Boyfriend*?

We've been through the whole confusing and yet exciting dating scene. However, there is yet another tough decision you might have to make about boys in middle school. (Believe us, it won't be the last!) This decision is about which is better: boy friend or boyfriend?

This can be a humongously difficult choice. Maybe you feel completely in love with a guy, and have a wonderful time with him no matter what you do, whether it's actually hanging out or just talking. You just never want to be without him! But maybe you're not really sure if you want to actually go out with him or just have him as this great pal that you can hang out with and talk to without worrying about how you act or look or whatever. It's a tough choice. Sometimes just the thrill of having a boyfriend is so cool and exciting that it's mind-boggling. But other times the joy of just having a wonderful guy friend is even more fabulous. So, thrill ride or true friend? There's no right answer. It's your choice, and you should really look inside. What do you want? Don't know? You're not alone.

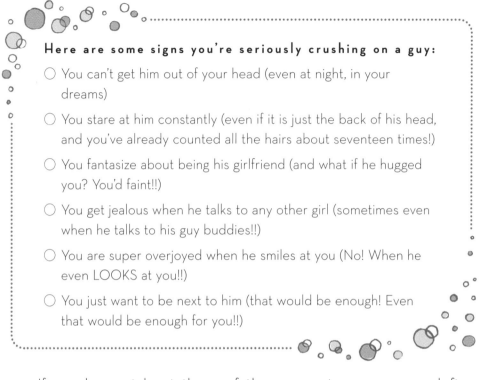

Here are some signs you're seriously crushing on a guy:

○ You can't get him out of your head (even at night, in your dreams)

○ You stare at him constantly (even if it is just the back of his head, and you've already counted all the hairs about seventeen times!)

○ You fantasize about being his girlfriend (and what if he hugged you? You'd faint!!)

○ You get jealous when he talks to any other girl (sometimes even when he talks to his guy buddies!!)

○ You are super overjoyed when he smiles at you (No! When he even LOOKS at you!!)

○ You just want to be next to him (that would be enough! Even that would be enough for you!!)

If you have at least three of those symptoms, you are definitely way into this guy and want to be his girlfriend—not just his friend.

But wait. Even though you're feeling all crazy in love, sometimes dating isn't the right thing to do. Like if Mr. Dreamboat has a girlfriend. Or if your Secret Love happens to be a teacher. (Sorry, babe, but he is off limits!!)

It may be that your Perfect Boyfriend is single. And he *is* available. But what about your friendship?? Would things get weird between you if you took things to another level? And how weird would it be when you broke up?? Chances are, in middle school, it will probably be very weird in either situation (probably both).

So:

* If Dreamboat is your really good friend, and you don't want to mess up anything with him,
* If things would just be too weird between the two of you (especially when you broke up), and
* If Mr. Right is off-limits (for example, he's a teacher, already dating someone, or two years younger than you, etc.) . . .

. . . then you should probably lay off. There are plenty of other puppies in the pound! They're just waiting for you to be their friend—after all, you don't *have* to have a boyfriend. So go out there and make some good guy friends! And maybe, if you find the right guy, and you think you're ready, you'll get a boyfriend, too. Just be smart about it, and have fun.

YOUR WORLD

Your Room

Rooms, rooms, rooms. It can be a very important subject when you start middle school, because at this point in your life you probably want your room to better represent who you are. A cool room that says "YOU" all over it is pretty awesome, so if you've grown out of the room you had when you were a little kid, this is the perfect time to start fresh.

Now, designing your room top to bottom is not something that all girls like doing! You should know that personalizing your room takes time. But it doesn't have to be difficult. If you collect things, that can be a good place to start. Find a way to display your stuffed animals, dolls, or other collections on a table or shelves. If you're not a collector, there are lots of easy ways to create a room that expresses who you are. That's because since your room represents *you*, whatever you think is cool will be perfect for your room! Starting to decorate can be as easy as putting up posters and pictures from magazines. Have a bulletin board for mementos; hang beaded curtains from your door frame; drape scarves or sarongs from your bedposts or hang them from the ceiling over your bed. Use craft paper to transform doors into a place where friends can sign their names or leave notes. Create a quiet corner with a beanbag or other comfy chair to read, draw, or think. Get a fun basket for dirty clothes (your mom will love that); cover boxes with decorative paper to store supplies. Rooms can be full of fun!! The most important thing is to be creative. That is the key to a fab-fab room.

HERE ARE SOME RESOURCES TO GET YOU STARTED!

Magazines to get pictures out of:

✶ YM　　✶ Teen People　　✶ Girls' Life　　✶ Cosmo Girl

Places to buy posters (most posters cost about $7 to $15):

✶ Tower Records (music posters)

✶ www.allposters.com

Books, magazines, stores and web sites to help with your room:

✶ FamilyFun magazine (pathetic name, good projects)

✶ Martha Stewart Living (okay, whatever, it's a good magazine!)

✶ Ikea (awesome, inexpensive furniture store. Go to www.Ikea.com.)

✶ Target.com (has teen room decorations)

✶ Pottery Barn's PBteen catalog or PBteen.com website

Books

Books are very cool. Whatever you're craving—history, fantasy, the facts, or the fake—we bet you a million dollars that there is a book about it. You may be saying, Books? Yuck. Who likes to read? Well, you may be used to watching television, but if you're as smart as we know you are, you'll take our advice: Get off of your hiney and pick up a book! Books are more than just words strung together. They're thoughts, opinions, stories, and new points of view that can pull you into entirely different worlds. Or that can help you figure out **your** world, because when you read books you often meet characters who think and feel the same way about things, including boys, friends, family—everything!—that you do! Go check out the Young Adult Fiction section of your library or bookstore, and we assure you that you will find a great book. (This section is approved by librarians.)

Movies

For you peeps who just **hate** books, it could be that you're a movie person. And if you're a person who does nothing but read, which is an independent activity, maybe you should go see that new chick flick that just came out with a few of your friends! The thing about movies is that they are group activities. When you are reading a good book, others can't enjoy it at the same time as you. But friends can enjoy a good film together, and that's what makes it a great, easy way to connect with pals, especially new pals. You automatically have something to talk about. Get your nose out of that book and go get some buttery popcorn, a soda, some friends, and some tickets!

Music

Music is a fabulous creation. Whether you want to dance, get pumped, do your math homework, or just chill with your friends, there is always a radio station you can tune to or a CD you can play. Music is great because it can help you get into or out of a mood. If you are sad, you can play some pop or rock that will get you happy and singing along. If you are excited and bouncy but you need to sit down and do your homework, you can pop in some calming classical music. If you just want to crawl into a hole, blast some hip-hop and dance along! No matter how you feel or want to feel, there is always some kind of music that you can pump up on your stereo. Find a kind of music you love and play it!

Fashion

Fashion is one of the few things in life that you can control. It's up to you to figure out how important fashion is to you. Once you do, another major question is: What is my style? This question should not be answered according to what is on the cover of the latest teen magazines, but according to what is inside you. Do you like bright colors or dark? Funky patterns or plain designs? It's all about what you like. Once you find your style, and for most people it can take a while, fashion can be a fun way to express yourself *and* cover your birthday suit!

Makeup Magic: Let the Real You Shine Through!

Not every girl is allowed to wear makeup in middle school (or wants to), but if you do wear makeup, there's one major thing for you to remember: You are unique. So despite whatever looks the fashion magazines tell you are "in" this season, those looks may not be right for you.

What always works, though, is going for a natural look, so that your one-of-a-kind beauty shines through! Makeup is not about hiding the real you. Rather, it's a tool to help you amp up your best features and accent the outer beauty that's already there (which is not nearly as important as the girl who's inside).

EASY STEPS FOR A NATURAL LOOK

1. Apply a little bit of eyeliner or mascara. To apply eyeliner (non-liquid), draw a thin line from the inside corner to the outside corner of your eye, as close to your eyelashes as possible. Be **very careful!** If you accidentally touch your eye, it could hurt **a lot**, which is why we recommend getting some advice/counseling from a trusted (older) female first before attempting to put on eyeliner. To apply mascara, start with your upper lashes. Starting at the base of your lashes (again, be very careful not to touch your eye), slowly sweep the brush up, toward the tips of your lashes. Do the same for your lower lashes, except sweep down.

2. Next are your lips. To get that "just stung by a bee" look, we recommend a clear or tinted gloss, which will bring out your natural tone and jet-puff your pout. To keep it from wearing away, apply a tiny bit of powder to your lips first. This will give your lip gloss something to stick to. If you don't want to accent your lips (maybe you have braces), try a matte-finish lip tint, which provides color without being shiny.

BEAUTIFUL!

YOUR BODY AND YOU

Body Image

Everyone in the world is different. We all have our own styles, tastes, and personalities, characteristics that make us special and unique. Even our bodies are unique because no two bodies are the same!

When you think about it this way, you realize that being you is totally cool because there's no on else in the whole wide world quite like you. It's pretty powerful knowing that no one else has your body or face. (Unless you have a twin or two! Chances are you don't, but if you do, that's super cool!)

The point is, sometimes you're happy to be you, every bit of you. But other times you don't want to look like you at all. You want to look like someone else that you think is prettier or taller

or skinnier or curvier than you are, like your best friend, who suddenly has hips and size 34C breasts! And hey, whoever said a girl couldn't dream? There's only one catch: No matter how much you wish it, at the end of the day you are still your fabulous self and not anybody else. So whenever you get bummed out over looks, think about this: We are all meant to look different from birth. It's genetics—you're meant to look exactly how you look because of that one-of-a-kind combination that comes from you being a product of your parents and their parents and *their* parents. And that's pretty cool!

So rather than wanting to wish away your brown eyes (oh, why can't they be blue??), think to yourself instead that you have the same warm, sparkling eyes as your grandpa who you love so much. How special is that? It's not always that easy, though, we know. So if all else fails, find a way to laugh about it—and get over it!

Boys and Your Bod

For many girls, middle school is a time of lots of physical changes. Your body is changing, and you're probably noticing that your friends' bodies are changing, too. Of course, boys go through their own changes, and just as you and your friends are noticing boys and their bodies a lot more, they're noticing you girls and *your* bodies more, too.

Sometimes you may be flattered by the attention. Sometimes, though, it may be embarrassing. Boys don't always know what to say about the changes in girls, and so some (wisely) decide not to comment at all. However, others may react by doing silly things like trying to snap your bra straps or even making comments about your breasts or your friend's butt. It's important for you to speak up right away to let a guy know he has gone too far (and if he does any of those things, he has!). He probably doesn't mean to hurt you, but it's still not okay for him to say or do anything that makes you uncomfortable, and he should know that.

On the dating side of boys and your body, it's really important to choose guys who like you for your personality and your brains—and not just for your hot bod. Who you are as a person means so much more than your looks, and if you choose to date, it should be with guys who appreciate that.

Fit to Be a Girl

Maybe you have a friend who's decided she wants to be a little bit skinnier, like the models on TV, so she's trying to lose weight by eating less. You feel the pressure to diet, too. What should you do?

First of all, your friend probably has no need to diet, and neither do you. Sometimes this is hard to realize because of the way the media portray women. You think that you should try to reach those warped ideals. But when you are young, your body is still developing. Of course you don't look like the women in magazines—you're not supposed to! Those body images are not healthy or realistic for girls, or for grown women either.

It is your job to be healthy, not ultra-skinny. To maintain and improve your health and appearance, the important thing is to exercise and eat well consistently, not to diet.

YOUR BODY AND YOU

Eating well means choosing healthfully prepared meals and snacks in sensibly sized portions. And exercise should be a fun part of your everyday life. It doesn't have to be a chore—and it shouldn't be! You can join the soccer team, walk or jog around your neighborhood, or even do yoga with your mom or a friend. Whatever physical activity you choose, it will help you build body muscle and strength. It can also be a big stress reliever that will help you concentrate better in class. Plus, it will give you something fun to do in your spare time. Just don't overdo it or push your body so hard that you get an injury. There are so many fun sports and physical activities that you will be able to find one you love and can really enjoy if you look. It's a great idea to exercise with a group of friends who can help keep you motivated and exercising regularly. Go for overall fitness instead of dieting, and you will see a lot of good results!

If you do have real concerns about your body, don't do anything dangerous like eating too little or exercising too much. Talk to your parents and your family doctor to come up with a plan together that will help you feel and look healthy and fit. No matter what, remember not to be hard on yourself and your body because you are still young and your body is changing and growing.

Here's what some girls had to say about their bodies:

JESSICA'S STORY

In the beginning of sixth grade, I didn't worry about what I looked like. I was only worried about if I would fit in. [But] as the time went by and my friends started getting bigger and fuller, I felt left out and scrawny. I started paying more and more attention to the women in the magazines and how "perfect" their bodies were and started wishing that my body was more like theirs. I started to watch what I ate a little more and wanted to exercise more to get that flat stomach I saw on the girls in the magazines. It was only after I learned that dieting and overexercising could make me really unhealthy that I stopped wanting to get skinny, because I was afraid to harm my body. My advice: You will be fine. Your body is nothing to worry about; it is a temple, so take good care of it! Your body is full of great surprises and if taken good care of will be your best friend for the rest of your life.

CASSANDRA'S STORY

I have always been a person who has had a good body image of myself. I've had my ups and downs about my appearance and weight, as many girls do. But over time I have come to one final decision about how to keep my body in a way that I can be happy about, and it is to exercise! Over time I have found that exercise is even more than just a way to get in shape. There is a mental and emotional part to it as well. When I exercise I feel good about myself, whether or not I lose weight. When I first started cross-country, I ran every day and became more in shape. Although I didn't lose any weight, I still felt much more confident about my body! Exercising is much more than a physical activity; it can change for the better the way you see and feel about your body!

MONIQUE'S STORY

I used to think about my looks all the time. And when I say all the time, I mean all the time! I was constantly noticing the way girls looked on TV and in magazines, and that all the best-liked girls in my class were tall and fair and skinny. It got to the point where I was even jealous of some of my closest friends because they looked the way I wished I looked! It took me a long time to real-ize I am who I am and that's that. I'm short and I'll never be tall. So what? And I'm dark and slim and just cute instead of light and super-skinny and drop-dead gorgeous. But that's okay, because I like the person I am. I'm a lot happier now that I like me.

Bras and You

Breasts come in all shapes and sizes. So do bras!! You may have large breasts, small breasts, or hardly any breasts. No matter what, there is a bra for you. The world of bras can be confusing at times. You may not know where to turn to buy a bra or who to turn to to buy it with!

It's important to know that not wanting a bra is normal, too. If you feel uncomfortable with the idea of wearing a bra, or you just don't feel like you need or want one, don't feel pressured to get one. It is totally cool to go free.

If you do want one, your mom is probably a Bra Veteran, so she can help. If you'd rather have someone who is closer to your age shop with you, ask your big sister or an older girlfriend. Or just have someone drive you to the mall where there are salespeople whose job it is to help fit you with a bra. They can find you one that trains, pushes up, flattens, or just looks good under a T-shirt—whatever suits your needs best.

BUYING A BRA

Always ask the people that work in that department for help! We know it may be embarrassing to ask someone you don't know for help with something you may be a little uncomfortable with, but it's their job to help people like you! The number of styles and sizes out there can be intimidating, but if you ask for help they can find the perfect bra for you.

A WORD ABOUT BRAS AND PARENTAL UNITS

Sometimes parents feel uncomfortable with their daughter buying bras, because it shows that their little girl is growing up! So if your parents say "No," don't whine over it. Instead, try to explain to them why you need or want one.

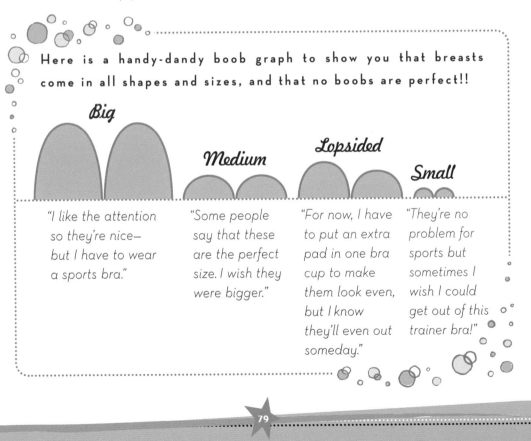

Here is a handy-dandy boob graph to show you that breasts come in all shapes and sizes, and that no boobs are perfect!!

Big

Medium

Lopsided

Small

"I like the attention so they're nice— but I have to wear a sports bra."

"Some people say that these are the perfect size. I wish they were bigger."

"For now, I have to put an extra pad in one bra cup to make them look even, but I know they'll even out someday."

"They're no problem for sports but sometimes I wish I could get out of this trainer bra!"

For the newly initiated, here's a handy technique for taking off your bra without taking off your shirt! It's a great trick for locker rooms.

HERE'S HOW!

1. Reach under your shirt to unclip your bra. (Or if you're really talented, you can unclip it through your shirt!)

2. If you're wearing a short-sleeve shirt or a tank top: Reach under your sleeves and grab one strap in each hand. Slip your hand underneath the strap, and push your whole arm through.

   If you're wearing a long-sleeve or three-quarter-sleeve shirt: Do almost the same thing, only after you unclip your bra, you'll need to really reeaach into each sleeve with the opposite hand and pull the straps down and off each arm (there's no need to take your arm out of the sleeve).

3. Now reach your hand up under the front of your shirt and pull your bra down. And then it's off (ta-da!)!!!

Periods! (The Real Deal)

Periods come at different times for everyone. Having it, or not having it, is nothing to be embarrassed about, because every woman gets it in her own time, a time that's right for her. If you haven't gotten your period yet but most your friends have, no worries! That's perfectly normal.

If you do have it, you should be proud! You are officially becoming a woman, and your body is now capable of having a baby—not any time soon, of course, because you are still really young and you aren't emotionally ready to have a child or to raise it. But one day you may want to have a baby, and that's why periods are a special experience.

When you get your period, you will be faced with a decision: Pads? Or tampons? Both pads and tampons are equally fine choices, but you may like one over the other. With tampons, you can go swimming or wear tighter clothing, but you have to insert it inside you, which some girls aren't comfortable with at first. Pads can be easily attached to your underwear and absorb just as well as tampons, but you're more limited as to what you wear. Whichever one you choose is A-okay; just remember to **change** your pad or tampon regularly to stay clean!

**Everyone experiences her first period differently.
Here are some personal experiences from our friends:**

CHARTREUSE'S STORY

I was the last one out of my friends to get my period. I was thirteen and in seventh grade when I first got it. It started when I was sitting in class. I was very uncomfortable, sitting in class, feeling exhausted. I ended up going home sick. A little later I was lying on my couch at home, not feeling too good. I went to the bathroom and noticed something red in my undies. I called for my mom and she informed me that I had just gotten my period. I was afraid to stand up, scared that if I did my period would pour out (even though it won't). My mom helped me get a pad and assured me that I would be fine. The next day I was so proud and told all of my friends.

LUCINDA'S STORY

I wasn't exactly sure what to expect, but I was sure excited! I was almost twelve years old and I'd gotten my period! Only one catch— I was at a retreat with my family, my best friend and her mom, and all of our parents' friends . . . and there were no pads in sight. My mom's friends offered me tampons, but I wasn't quite ready yet. (I'm still not. . .) When I first told my mom, she was so excited and proud! My mom gathered everyone in the retreat—all her friends, women and men—and had them make a circle around me under the stars. And then, in front of everyone, she announced, "Today, my daughter became a woman!" I was so embarrassed!! Everyone was really cool about it, and now I look back and laugh! But at the time, all I can remember is staring wide-eyed at my best friend and frantically mouthing, "Get me out of here!!"

MYRTLE'S STORY

My thirteenth birthday is a day which will live in my memories forever. It was both scary and exciting. I was at my dad's house for my birthday, and when I woke up I knew something was not quite right. A moment later I knew what was different. I had gotten my period! I WAS A WOMAN!! I was so excited. I had looked so forward to getting it and finally on my birthday it had come! As I thought about it, I suddenly got a sinking feeling in my stomach. My dad didn't have any pads or tampons, and neither did I! I didn't know what to do—my mom was away and wouldn't be home for another couple of days. I was too embarrassed to tell my dad, so I had to fashion pads from toilet paper and tissue. I made do with that until my mom got home and took me to buy supplies. It all turned out okay, I look back and wish I had told my dad. It's nothing to hide, and my dad (like most dads) would have just tried his best to understand.

ALICIA'S STORY

I consider the day I got my period as not very exciting. When I was in seventh grade, I got it with no problems. It was a regular Saturday and I was at home hanging out. I went to the bathroom (cuz I needed to pee!) and noticed red blood in my underpants. I told my mom and she gave me a tampon. I used a tampon no problem and went on with my everyday life. Getting my period for the first time was not very dramatic, as it can be for some girls. Getting your period is a totally normal thing, and the experience can be that way, too.

Turning Thirteen

Turning thirteen is a really big milestone in your life. Good-bye little girl, hello, womanhood! Even if you're not turning thirteen for a while, you should still be prepared! Now is the time for you to start thinking about who you are, and who you want to be when you are a teenager. Are there goals you want to work toward—things you want to have accomplished before this big year? What do you need to do to be prepared for your up-and-coming teenager-hood?

Thirteen is when you are officially a teenager and you have much more expected of you. On the downside, no more discounts at the restaurants and no more cheap movie tickets. On the upside, more privileges, more parties, more everything! Younger kids will probably look up to you and you will have to set a good example for all of the little ones down there.

One very, very important part of turning thirteen is the **party!** You need to throw a really fun, exciting, cool party that everyone will want to come to! Make it full of your personality and it's sure to be a birthday you'll never forget!

On a completely serious level, a really important part of approaching your teenage years is knowing your boundaries and sticking to them. Be strong against people or things that try to influence you to do things you don't want to do. At any time in your life you do not have to smoke, do drugs, have sex, or any of that stuff. If all of your friends are plucking their eyebrows or shaving their legs or dating, that does not mean that you have to do it, too. You can do it if you want, but you don't *have* to.

Just Say NO!

Saying no is very important. If someone says, "Do you want a smoke?" you don't want to say yes! When you think about it for even a second, it's a no-brainer: You say NO to things like smoking and taking drugs because if you say yes, you're putting your health, and even your life, in danger. How pathetic is that? Very. Sometimes it's not easy to say no when you're facing peer pressure from peeps that ask, "Why not? Are you scared?" Or "Oh, I see. The wittle baby is a wittle scared!" and then burst out laughing. Lots of people crack under this pressure because they want to be cool and popular. But if you're smart, you'll just say something like, "No, I'm not scared, I want to live for a few years, thank you very much. But I see you don't want to," and then just walk away.

If someone says, "Do you want to have sex?" (And you are how old? Like, um, thirteen?) would you say yes? Uh, no. Unless you want to lose your virginity, and risk getting pregnant and having a kid in junior high, or getting some horrible disease. Yeah, that is really cool—not. You want to say . . . (okay girl, what's the magic word?)

Nnnnnnoooooooo!!!!!!!!!!

Or just NO. That's it. NO is a really strong word, and when you say it like you mean it, it means, "I don't want to do that, no way!" You should always say no if that's what feels right to you, even though friends may think you're scared and uncool or try to pressure or force you. You should care about friends, and your social life, but your top priority is **yourself!**

GOOD-BYE AND GOOD LUCK!

Now that we have passed on our super cool knowledge, you're ready to catch the loads of school, boy, family, and super special friendship issues that middle school throws your way. Middle school is a jungle, yes, but take it from us: It's much more fun than that. In fact, think of it as being like a big theme park: There will be roller-coaster rides, haunted houses of terror, even clowns. But whatever chills and thrills are in store for you, you can handle it. You can do anything! We're always here for you in spirit, and when that's not enough, you've got this book. **Good luck!**

Hugs and kisses,

Sara, Sarah, Alex, Maria, and Miriam

MY MIDDLE SCHOOL NOTES

From the Desk of

....

(your name here)

Once you start middle school and get into the swing of things, you'll find yourself growing in exciting and unexpected ways! You will learn a lot of new things about yourself and discover you can do things you didn't think you'd be able to do. You'll even look back on some of your old worries and fears and laugh about them! Because back then you wondered if you'd ever be able to deal. But now you know you definitely can!

Here's a place to record your top discoveries about yourself, about who you are and what you can do, now that you're in middle school!

The best thing about middle school:

....

....

....

....

....

....

The worst thing about middle school:

....

....

....

....

....

Challenges I have in middle school that I didn't have
in grade school:

....

....

....

....

....

Something that scared me at first about going to middle school—but doesn't scare me anymore!

....

....

....

....

....

What I'm learning about myself now that I'm in middle school:

....

....

....

....

....

My most triumphant middle-school moment:

....

....

....

....

....

My most embarrassing middle-school moment . . .
and how I got over it!

....
....
....
....
....

Something about middle school that I never expected:

....
....
....
....
....

Advice I would give to someone starting middle school:

....
....
....
....
....